Camille Abroad

Jennifer Lagier

FUTURECYCLE PRESS

www.futurecycle.org

Published by FutureCycle Press
Lexington, Kentucky, USA

ISBN 978-1-942371-19-9

"Good girls go to heaven, bad girls go everywhere."
—Unknown

For all the bad girls
who grow up to be dangerous women

Contents

Sparring With Beatnik Ghosts

Camille debates which shade of black
she should wear to the reading.
Calculates how much cleavage
would irritate other women,
shake her out of a slump,
seduce a new lover.

Applies ebony eyeliner,
a thick layer of Erase
to efface the dark circles.
Paints her nails red.
Slithers into tight leggings.
Rehearses her repertoire
of witty ripostes, cynical topics.

The featured poet
hits on her five minutes
after she arrives.
Drops names,
invites her to
spend the evening beside him.

She smiles as he hands her
a fresh bottle of vodka.

Rerun

Camille has a ring-side seat
at the end of the bar
in the No Mercy Saloon.
From here, she can watch
over-the-hill players as they ply
desperate divorcées in their forties,
twentysomething airheads
with umbrella drinks.

She has played a starring role
in similar romantic farces,
decides to sit this one out,
relax and observe.
Can mime common pick-up lines
and flirty responses.

Sees an older man on the
opposite side of the counter.
He too is taking a breather,
enjoying the movie.
Catches her eye, tips his glass,
smiles in amusement.

She feels something stir,
knocks back the last of her wine.
Already knows how it ends
but figures "what the hell...."
Accepts his kind offer of refill.

Same Old Movie

Camille has been down this road before.
Recognizes all the red flags.
He is distant, cool.
Lost his appetite.
Hasn't wanted sex in months.
Talks less and less.
Works all night at the office.
Won't answer emails or phone.
Says it's nothing personal.
Just going through a phase.
Wants to be by himself.

Camille is out of patience,
sick of the same old routine.
She imagines cutting her losses.
Frosting her hair, packing a bag.
Climbing on a plane.
She'd welcome new scenery,
fresh start in a warm, foreign land,
meeting no end of fascinating,
sensual, intellectual men.

Expatriot

Camille breezes through security,
unpacks her laptop, checks email,
Facebook, from an airport café.
The trim waiter brings hot chowder,
an icy mimosa, offers tempting desserts.

In an hour, she'll lift off from San Francisco,
wave goodbye to parched California:
crowded cookie cutter houses,
empty reservoirs,
snowless Sierras.

At the boarding gate,
she unclenches,
imagines a clean slate,
reinvented reality,
herself starting over.

Departure from Been-there-and-done-it-to-death.
Destination: Adventure. Possibility. Barcelona. Madrid.

Alicante

Camille wanders wonderland byways:
dizzying Paseo de la Explanada de España,
secret plazas, their kiosks and fountains,
skinny alley decorated with fantastical mushrooms.

She discovers tiny cafés serving pizza and tapas.
Treats herself to Spanish beer, then flan
complemented by cups of espresso.
Returns the smile of a dark Spaniard who winks,
generously foots the bill for her sangria.

Watches beautiful men holding hands,
sipping champagne at a yacht harbor bistro.
Spends the night in a penthouse overlooking
high-rise apartments, twitching ocean,
flickering streetlights.

From between black satin sheets,
she imagines Dos Passos, Hemingway, Stein;
dreams of matadors, bullfights,
an Iberian world filled with fiery lovers.

Carne

While in Spain, Camille renounces
her vegetarian past, craves meat
in every form, morning and night.
Salivates over salami, thin prosciutto slices,
grows wet at the sight of foil-wrapped ham.

Crisp bacon tempts,
weans her from breakfast yogurt.
Siren song of steak and sangria for lunch.
By dinner, her appetite is reduced
to bruschetta sprinkled with chorizo,
a bit of green salad, shards of hard cheese.

All night she fantasizes flesh in many forms:
succulent pork, mouth-watering beef.
Sleeps soundly, lost in carnal dreams.

Madrid

Policía in blue uniforms twirling black mausers
form a mandatory reception line leading into the train terminal
where Camille is divested of purse and belt, subjected to a full-body scan.

In the coach car, passengers sit two by two.
An attendant pushes a squeaky cart down the narrow aisle,
dispenses espresso, newspapers, travel advice.

Green fields, leafless vineyards, graffiti flash by.
A gravel-voiced matron shouts *¡Hola!*
conversing at high decibel on her oversized phone.

Civil guardsmen on every corner recall bloody terrorist bombings.
Mimes and street performers command crammed Madrid plazas,
banter with tourists, beg for coins and applause.

At the Prada, cathedrals, museums, more soldiers swarm.
Camille finds a peaceful table under pink blossoming trees.
Sips wine in a tiny demilitarized zone.

Mimo

Camille has known her share of changelings.
This silver Spaniard with metallic stage props
simply one more performance artist
camouflaged by imaginative makeup.
He postures, plays to the crowd,
donation can before his podium,
aggressively shilling for money.

The man has neither humility nor shame.
Stares and smirks, intuits exactly
what Camille is thinking
as she flings a small coin,
pauses to appraise
his trim, wiry physique.

Camille is ready
to reinvent her persona.
Vows to diet, try lipo,
inject botox, some filler.
Emulate a chameleon,
craft a new face and body.

Plaza de Major

It's barely 11 a.m., and the plaza is crowded.
Camille wanders among hustlers,
acrobats, mimes, *policía* in blue uniforms
who cradle black rifles.

Pale heroin addicts sprawl against sunlit walls.
Outside cafés, every table is crowded.
Harried waitresses carry baskets of bread,
Spanish omelets, cups of fragrant espresso.

A bridal party spills from a nearby chapel,
so immature they look like children in costumes.
Camille has explored this option,
has no desire for tradition or husband.

She is still discovering who she is,
what she can achieve; wants to learn
other languages, savor
alternative continents, cultures.

Negra y Ángel

A dark Iberian angel leads Camille
past her comfort zone,
through a canyon of vintage apartments,
along cracked, slanting sidewalks
on her way to antique city center,
then to the sea.

Around her, spray-painted gang slogans,
intricate graffiti artwork.
Children wave paper streamers on sticks.
Elderly men and women pull shopping carts
or hold leashes tethered to small, ratty dogs.

Outside each *tienda,*
black-stockinged shop girls cluster,
clutching lit cigarettes;
gesture and share juicy gossip;
blow blue smoke into brisk breeze,
howling with laughter.

Beach Esplanade

Camille explores the old town beach promenade.
Dizzying bands of cream, green, and rust tiles wriggle
between inns, marketplace booths, white swath of sand.
Before 10 a.m., a thin stream of curious tourists.
Here and there, an elderly couple walking their dog.

She marvels at pastel high-rise apartments—
their wrought iron balconies floating gardens
of scarlet geranium, vivid nasturtium—
imagines what it must look like at night,
boisterous crowds traversing patterned path,
waving ever-present cigarettes, clutching cold beers.

From her café table abutting the esplanade,
she sips potent espresso, watches joggers,
a shirtless rollerblader with muscular legs,
and sighs at the sight of his rippling abs.

Procesión

At Plaza de Santa Maria, Camille stumbles
upon a colorful, noisy parade.
Women blow bagpipes, click castanets.
Vested men wave lettered banners,
strum their wooden guitars.

Tourists and shoppers merge
with exuberant musicians and marchers.
Diners spill onto sidewalks
from dim, cave-like cafés.

Camille leans against a lamppost,
nods to a passing cleric
who glares, gives her the once-over,
makes the evil eye sign.

One vivacious gent pauses, winks,
mimes holding a wine glass.
They rendezvous in a nearby bistro
where she welcomes seduction,
wakes to luminous sunrise.

Tapas y Tequila

After stumbling into the midst of a church procession,
Camille, who is allergic to piety, craves an antidote to religion.
Heads to Plaza Santa Barbara and her favorite café.
Orders tapas and tequila, discretely settles into a nook,
eavesdrops on couples canoodling at dark corner tables.

Bartender Luis knows her weaknesses, serves local scandal
in lisping Spanish over espresso, sangria.
Chalks today's paella specials on blackboards
hung from ancient stone walls at the foot of a staircase.
Croons sexily with music videos, holds out a hand,
invites her to join him.

"When in Spain," she thinks, knocking back a shot.
Grinds her way to the dance floor.

Emigrada

Camille considers renouncing American citizenship,
relocating to a funky Alicante flat
overlooking cafés and pocket parks,
a glimpse of silvery ocean.

She imagines morning excursions
tethered to the leash of a fat, spoiled Chihuahua,
casual flirtation with lively gentlemen
still in possession of that certain sparkle.

Hers would be the wrought iron balcony
spilling red geraniums, after-dark laughter.
She envisions intimacy on her terrace, sipping wine
beside the evening's hot lover.

Rainstorm

As Camille dejectedly packs her suitcase,
the Alicante skies open, wash ancient buildings
and congested streets with silver downpour.
Thunder grumbles, wallops rain from storm clouds,
matches her conflicting emotions, dark mood.

The last day in Spain and there's still
so many unexplored cantinas,
but her return flight to California
lifts off just after dawn.

Pink trees shower wet streets
with wind-propelled blossoms.
She digs out the passport, breaks down her computer.

This time tomorrow, she'll clear customs in Madrid,
then again in Chicago; suffer re-entry jet lag;
sleep overnight, if she can, in San Francisco.

Camille reviews names in her phonebook,
friends with whom to share a glass of wine,
exaggerated stories of lewd adventures.

Sliced Like Pie

Camille now has separate doctors
for each body part, disease, mental dysfunction.
Divides her life between free-spirit bohemian,
recovering lover, responsible daughter.

Is energetic in early morning:
power-walks miles of trail,
invites her poetry muse
to join her for coffee.

By mid-afternoon she begins to sag,
craves a long, quiet nap
with two sleepy dogs
on a comfortable sofa.

She becomes what she has always feared:
a difficult, middle-aged woman.
Transforms from sexy, lively dynamo
into cranky curmudgeon.

Shot to Hell

It's like putting lipstick on a pig,
Camille thinks, painting cracked toenails.
Her hand shakes, smears scarlet
onto dry skin where it doesn't belong.
She has trouble bending—a growing
fat roll circling her belly gets in the way.
She'd laugh, but that would cause her
to pee, despite thousands of kegels.

At the mirror, she beholds a blurry image
that looks like a younger version
of her elderly mother.
Leans in to pluck chin hairs,
count the new wrinkles.
Sighs as she remembers
clutching a man between thighs
now veined and flabby.
Misses seduction on cool sheets
during sultry Mediterranean summers.

No Way Out

Camille spies an old lover
sitting across the room
in her favorite café.
He huddles in a corner,
scowls at the menu,
seems dejected, fatigued.

She remembers drunken Fridays,
fondling one another, sharing shots
in discreet, sleazy bars.
Stoned lust followed by hours
of sexual capers.

Now a gold band strangles his finger.
She imagines him in bed by nine,
swaddled in geezer pajamas,
banished to his side
of chaste marital mattress.

Allergic to commitment,
she misses his hands, camaraderie;
wonders why she aches.

So Much Has Gone

Camille contemplates a gray pubic hair.
Critiques her naked self in the full-length mirror:
belly and breasts beginning to sag,
silver laparoscopy scars,
what was once golden and taut
now drooping, wrinkled, or flat.

It's confusing—she feels nineteen inside.
Her nipples still stand at attention,
face flushes, juices flow
when aroused by a man.

She's knows who she is,
what she wants out of life.
Then, just as she hits her peak,
this goddamned body
develops a mind of its own,
starts falling apart.

Everything Just Stays the Same

The white male talking head
on Camille's television gushes
over Bruce Jenner's sex change,
proclaims once she transitions
to Caitlin, she can serve
as a strong voice for women.

Camille picks her jaw up off the floor,
wonders what attribute qualifies Cait
to speak for generations
of marginalized females.
Is this a role she ever
wanted, envisioned?

News anchors fixate
on her altered appearance,
couture and makeup.
She is now officially
one more gal
to be judged solely
on the basis of looks
instead of actual substance.

This Place Has Found Us

Camille watches The Donald
cozying up to Sarah Palin,
degenerating MILF,
maverick moron,
Tea Party darling.

It's amazing that much
willful disinformation
in a confined space
doesn't implode the skulls
of cheering fans
who gather around them.

Camille craves tokes
to erase coming months
of campaign chatter,
political pandering.

Regrets going dry
at a time when
she desperately needs
a prolonged bender,
then sustained blackout.

Sadly Sane

Camille is sick
of being sensible,
paying bills,
dumping trash,
buying groceries,
cooking dinner,
doing laundry.

She wants to resurrect
her old inner hippie,
turn on, tune in, drop out.
Less work and more play.
Poetry, music, meditation,
being naked in nature.

Adulthood isn't
what she had expected,
freedom cancelled
by unending projects.
She pines for playmates
to inspire delinquency,
join her rebellion.

Don't Lament Lost Youth

Camille dons a fuchsia smock,
reclines in a leather chair
as the nurse scrubs alcohol
into her face, explains
upcoming procedures.

First, botox injected here and there
to remove forehead furrows,
a jab at the end of each brow
to lift sagging eyelids.

Next, topical anesthetic,
then Novocain shots,
thin lips rejuvenated
by syringes loaded with filler.

The specialist inserts a needle,
lifts raw flesh to encourage
growth of new collagen
under each wrinkle.

She emerges with a pouty mouth,
no marionette creases,
but she'll need ice packs and arnica
to minimize swelling and bruising.

Eventually, she'll invest
in coolsculpting treatments
to freeze away stubborn fat,
restore taut chin, neck and belly.

Camille endures pain
to emulate youth.
Spends a fortune to purchase
fleeting Frankenstein beauty.

Mane Events

A chubby toddler,
Camille possessed a few golden wisps.
When the 1950s pixie cut grew out,
Her mother wove thin hair
into tight, skinny braids.

By the early 60s, she wore
bleached, feathered highlights
over a ratted beehive
to accompany poodle skirts, fluffy slips.

During the Summer of Love,
Camille smoked dope, visited Haight-Ashbury
clad in Nehru jacket,
flat, ironed locks and leather headband,
paisley bell-bottomed pants.

The 70s brought women's lib
and a messy divorce.
She flaunted a blonde afro,
went braless beneath skimpy tank tops
and peg-legged tiny jeans.

During late 80s, early 90s,
she traded classic pageboy
for moussed punk spikes,
message tee shirts,
anti-war picket signs.

Now Camille wrestles faded cowlicks,
refuses to consider blue tresses, phony wig,
pays a professional to paint auburn streaks
through her anemic mane,
resurrect vanished youth.

Each Night Counts

Camille unpacks, pops a beer,
settles into a tiny cabin
deep within redwoods.
Spreads her books and laptop
on an oak kitchen table.

Waves at the sexy, aging hippie
outside her window
who pours two glasses of Pinot Noir,
heads toward the hot tub.

Camille tosses her cutoffs and
tee shirt onto the sofa,
sighs as she slides
into hot roiling water,
lets her naked body
shed its aches.

Feels his hands
and sudden hardness.
Imagines juicy, mature pleasures ahead.
Welcomes him into this chapter
of her Russian River adventure.

AARP Booty Call

Camille meets Roy at Applebee's
for an Early Bird Dinner.
They connected online at SeniorPeople.com,
found each other's profile intriguing.
Enjoyed the "before" and "after" photos,
battle wounds of aging.

Both still have their own teeth,
a sense of humor,
raging libidos.
Qualify for AARP discounts
at restaurants, motels.
Love to eat, drink, and travel.

After more dates,
they share a bed, discover
they can laugh at arthritic hips,
stretch marks, sagging boobs,
Cialis and wrinkles.

All that's missing
is flexibility, stamina—
nothing yoga can't cure.

Raging Grannies

Camille constructs her picket sign,
demands an immediate end to the war on women,
deplores craven male politicians who legislate
against Planned Parenthood,
access to contraception, affordable housing.

She is fed up with guys who discriminate,
call themselves compassionate-conservative Christians.
They fund black ops, promote militarism,
destroy watersheds, rape forests.

Camille has had it with the status quo,
calls out corrupt public figures,
takes her cause to the streets,
stops traffic as she shouts,
"Get Your Rosaries Off Our Ovaries!"
Supports the sisterhood,
hangs with radical grannies.

Camille at the Medicare Workshop

As the consultant
draws on his flip chart,
blathers on
about drug plans,
deductibles,
Camille practices
five sets of kegels.
Craves margaritas
or martinis,
maybe a nooner.
Wishes her damp panties
were a reaction to arousal
rather than laughter.
Observes saggy old women,
pot-bellied men,
in the chair rows around her.
Wonders why 65 juicy years
have ambushed her patience,
tautness, libido.
Blows off this workshop.
Sneaks out the back door.
Fires up a big doobie.

Acknowledgments

The author is grateful for the editorial assistance provided by Charles Rammelkamp, Kate Aver Avraham, and Laura Bayless.

Abbey: "Sadly Sane"
Dead Snakes: "This Place Has Found Us"
Dead Snakes and *misfitmagazine.com:* "Expatriot," "Carne," "Mimo," "Madrid," "Beach Esplanade," "Tapas y Tequila"
misfitmagazine.net: "Alicante," "Emigrada," "Rainstorm"
Silver Birch Press, My Mane Memories Theme: "Mane Events"
The Potomac: "Same Old Movie," "So Much Has Gone," "Sparring With Beatnik Ghosts," "Camille at the Medicare Workshop"
Your One Phone Call: "Shot to Hell"

Cover artwork by Gene McCormick; cover and interior book design by Diane Kistner; Calisto MT text and Belotta titling

About FutureCycle Press

FutureCycle Press is dedicated to publishing lasting English-language poetry books, chapbooks, and anthologies in both print-on-demand and Kindle ebook formats. Founded in 2007 by long-time independent editor/publishers and partners Diane Kistner and Robert S. King, the press incorporated as a nonprofit in 2012. A number of our editors are distinguished poets and writers in their own right, and we have been actively involved in the small press movement going back to the early seventies.

The FutureCycle Poetry Book Prize and honorarium is awarded annually for the best full-length volume of poetry we publish in a calen-dar year. Introduced in 2013, our Good Works projects are anthologies devoted to issues of universal significance, with all proceeds donated to a related worthy cause. Our Selected Poems series highlights contempo-rary poets with a substantial body of work to their credit; with this series we strive to resurrect work that has had limited distribution and is now out of print.

We are dedicated to giving all of the authors we publish the care their work deserves, making our catalog of titles the most diverse and distinguished it can be, and paying forward any earnings to fund more great books.

We've learned a few things about independent publishing over the years. We've also evolved a unique, resilient publishing model that allows us to focus mainly on vetting and preserving for posterity poetry collections of exceptional quality without becoming overwhelmed with bookkeeping and mailing, fundraising activities, or taxing editorial and production "bubbles." To find out more about what we are doing, come see us at www.futurecycle.org.

www.ingramcontent.com/pod-product-compliance
Lightning Source LLC
Chambersburg PA
CBHW060046050426
42448CB00012B/3131